STUDY GUIDE

CHURCH HURT

Copyright © 2025 by André Butler

Published by AVAIL

All rights reserved. No portion of this book may be reproduced, stored in a retrieval system, or transmitted in any form or by any means—electronic, mechanical, photocopy, recording, scanning, or other—except for brief quotations in critical reviews or articles, without prior written permission of the author.

Unless otherwise specified, all Scripture quotations are taken from the Holy Bible, New Living Translation, copyright © 1996, 2004, 2015 by Tyndale House Foundation. Used by permission of Tyndale House Publishers, Inc., Carol Stream, Illinois 60188. All rights reserved. | Scripture quotations marked MSG are taken from THE MESSAGE, copyright © 1993, 1994, 1995, 1996, 2000, 2001, 2002 by Eugene H. Peterson. Used by permission of NavPress. All rights reserved. Represented by Tyndale House Publishers, Inc. | Scripture quotations marked NKJV are taken from the New King James Version®. Copyright © 1982 by Thomas Nelson. Used by permission. All rights reserved.

For foreign and subsidiary rights, contact the author.

Cover design by: Sara Young
Cover photo by: Kai Davis

ISBN: 978-1-964794-90-7   1 2 3 4 5 6 7 8 9 10
Printed in the United States of America

STUDY GUIDE

CHURCH HURT

ANDRÉ BUTLER

CONTENTS

CHAPTER 1.	**Church Hurt HURTS**	6
CHAPTER 2.	**My Healing Story**	10
CHAPTER 3.	**Is Church Hurt a New Phenomenon?**	16
CHAPTER 4.	**Who's Behind Church Hurt?**	22
CHAPTER 5.	**God Cares**	28
CHAPTER 6.	**Let God Heal You**	34
CHAPTER 7.	**Let It Go!**	40
CHAPTER 8.	**Don't Pick the Scab**	46
CHAPTER 9.	**Time to Grow**	52
CHAPTER 10.	**The Church Is Full of Hypocrites!**	58
CHAPTER 11.	**The Yellow Brick Road**	64
CHAPTER 12.	**Is Church Really Necessary?**	70
CHAPTER 13.	**Is Church Attendance Optional?**	76
CHAPTER 14.	**I Don't Need a Leader**	82
CHAPTER 15.	**It Happens**	88
CHAPTER 16.	**Friendly Fire**	94
CHAPTER 17.	**Church Isn't Wack**	100
CHAPTER 18.	**For Pastors Only**	106
CHAPTER 19.	**Church Hurt and Preachers' Kids**	112
CHAPTER 20.	**Church Hurt and Family Ministry**	118
CHAPTER 21.	**When a Leader Fails**	124
CHAPTER 22.	**It's Time to Move Past Church Hurt**	130

CHURCH HURT

IT'S TIME TO HEAL

ANDRÉ BUTLER

CHAPTER 1

CHURCH HURT HURTS

Sometimes, people don't realize that church leaders also experience church hurt.

REVIEW, REFLECT, AND RESPOND

READING TIME As you read Chapter 1: "Church Hurt HURTS" in *Church Hurt*, review, reflect on, and respond to the text by answering the following questions.

Have you ever felt misunderstood or treated differently in church because of who someone thought you were—rather than who you really are? How has that shaped your willingness to connect in a church setting?

_____
_____
_____
_____
_____
_____
_____
_____

When have you experienced hurt in church that came from unmet expectations—someone not being there for you, leadership failure, or broken trust? What do you still carry from that experience?

_____
_____
_____
_____
_____
_____
_____
_____

I share about people using me to get close to my father. Have you ever been used or overlooked in a church context for someone else's gain? How did that affect your sense of belonging?

_____
_____
_____
_____
_____
_____
_____
_____
_____
_____

The chapter makes a powerful point that even great churches with great people still hurt others. Has the expectation of perfection in a church ever made your pain worse or harder to name?

_____
_____
_____
_____
_____
_____
_____
_____
_____
_____

What hidden pain have you carried silently because you assumed no one—especially a pastor—would understand it?

___

Jesus experienced the betrayal and abandonment of His own followers. How does that truth challenge or comfort you in the way you've processed your own church wounds?

___

CHAPTER 2

MY HEALING STORY

It is impossible to heal when you continue to think and talk about what happened to you.

REVIEW, REFLECT, AND RESPOND

READING TIME As you read Chapter 2: "My Healing Story" in *Church Hurt*, review, reflect on, and respond to the text by answering the following questions.

Have you ever had to "show up" spiritually while feeling broken inside? What did that cost you?

_____
_____
_____
_____
_____
_____
_____
_____

In your own words, what does it mean to "pray through" your pain? What does that look like practically?

_____
_____
_____
_____
_____
_____
_____
_____

> *"And now, dear brothers and sisters, one final thing. Fix your thoughts on what is true, and honorable, and right, and pure, and lovely, and admirable. Think about things that are excellent and worthy of praise."*
>
> Philippians 4:8 (NLT)

Consider the scripture above and answer the following questions:

When have you found yourself dwelling on the injustice of a situation rather than releasing it to God? What effect has that had on your emotional or spiritual health?

_____
_____
_____
_____
_____
_____
_____
_____

What mental "channel" do you need to intentionally change when your thoughts drift back to what was done to you? What could you choose to think about instead?

_____
_____
_____
_____
_____
_____
_____
_____

What situation in your life have you been begging God to fix quickly, and what would it look like to "cheerfully endure" instead?

_____
_____
_____
_____
_____
_____
_____
_____
_____
_____
_____

Who are the godly friends in your life that you need to open up to, even if it feels vulnerable or awkward?

_____
_____
_____
_____
_____
_____
_____
_____
_____
_____
_____

What story have you repeated—not to heal, but to stay angry or feel justified? How has holding onto that version of events shaped your heart, your relationships, or your ability to move forward?

_____
_____
_____
_____
_____
_____
_____
_____
_____
_____

Where are you still seeking justice more than you're seeking peace?

_____
_____
_____
_____
_____
_____
_____
_____
_____
_____
_____

The chapter ends with a reminder that we will stand before God for our response, not their actions. How does that truth challenge the way you've handled recent offenses?

_____
_____
_____
_____
_____
_____
_____
_____
_____
_____
_____
_____

CHAPTER 3

IS CHURCH HURT A NEW PHENOMENON?

Church hurt has been a part of Satan's playbook since the beginning

---

REVIEW, REFLECT, AND RESPOND

READING TIME As you read Chapter 3: "Is Church Hurt a New Phenomenon?" in *Church Hurt*, review, reflect on, and respond to the text by answering the following questions.

Church fighting is compared to sibling rivalry in a family. How have you seen "family-level" closeness in church lead to both deep connection and deep conflict? How do you navigate the difference?

_____
_____
_____
_____
_____
_____
_____
_____

In Acts 6, the early church responded to discrimination with action and resolution. When have you seen inequity or favoritism create hurt in a church—and how was (or wasn't) it addressed?

_____
_____
_____
_____
_____
_____
_____
_____

> *"But if you are always biting and devouring one another, watch out! Beware of destroying one another."*
> Galatians 5:15 (NLT)

Consider the scripture above and answer the following questions:

When have you witnessed or participated in "biting and devouring" behavior within your church community? What damage did it cause—internally or externally?

_____
_____
_____
_____
_____
_____
_____

Paul warns that unchecked division can lead to destruction. What steps do you personally need to take to stop contributing to relational tension in the church—whether through criticism, avoidance, gossip, or silence?

_____
_____
_____
_____
_____
_____
_____

The split between Paul and Barnabas shows how even strong spiritual leaders can fall out. Has a leadership conflict ever shaken your faith or trust in God's people? How have you processed that disillusionment?

_____
_____
_____
_____
_____
_____
_____
_____
_____
_____

Imagine being John Mark—knowing that your past failure caused a ministry team to divide. Have you ever been the one whose actions or mistakes caused pain or division? How does that memory affect the way you judge those who've hurt you in church?

_____
_____
_____
_____
_____
_____
_____
_____
_____
_____

CHURCH HURT: STUDY GUIDE

The chapter reminds us that Satan has long used division and jealousy to attack God's people. Where have you seen the enemy succeed in using these tactics in your own story or faith community?

_____
_____
_____
_____
_____
_____
_____
_____
_____
_____

Where in your life has church hurt stalled your spiritual momentum or made you second-guess your calling?

_____
_____
_____
_____
_____
_____
_____
_____
_____
_____
_____

The Greek widows in Acts 6 likely felt invisible. When have you felt overlooked or undervalued in a church setting—and what healing still needs to happen from that moment?

_____
_____
_____
_____
_____
_____
_____
_____
_____
_____

John Mark's story ends in redemption—but only after time passed and perspectives changed. Who might need your forgiveness or a second chance—even if you're not ready to reconcile fully?

_____
_____
_____
_____
_____
_____
_____
_____
_____
_____

CHAPTER 4

WHO'S BEHIND CHURCH HURT?

God does not have to use Satan's weapons to teach you His lessons.

REVIEW, REFLECT, AND RESPOND

READING TIME As you read Chapter 4: "Who's Behind Church Hurt?" in *Church Hurt*, review, reflect on, and respond to the text by answering the following questions.

Who have you been blaming for your pain without recognizing the real spiritual source behind it?

___

The chapter says Satan sends persecution or tribulation specifically to steal God's Word from your heart. What Word or promise were you beginning to believe before church hurt tried to snatch it away?

___

> *"But reach out and take away everything he has, and he will surely curse you to your face!"* Job 1:11 (NLT)

Consider the scripture above and answer the following questions:

According to Satan's accusation, Job's loyalty to God was conditional. How do you tend to respond spiritually when things fall apart in your life?

_____
_____
_____
_____
_____
_____
_____

Have you ever felt tempted to walk away from God because of pain inflicted by church people? What did you say or believe about God in that moment? How did that reaction play into the enemy's strategy?

_____
_____
_____
_____
_____
_____
_____

Think about a time you felt offended, resentful, or angry right after a spiritual breakthrough. Looking back, how do you see the enemy working to derail your growth?

___

This chapter challenges the idea that storms are sent by God to make us stronger. How has believing that lie shaped the way you process hardship, loss, or church wounds?

___

When have you blamed God for the actions of His people—and how has that misdirected blame affected your relationship with Him?

_____
_____
_____
_____
_____
_____
_____
_____
_____
_____

The chapter describes God confronting Job for trying to justify himself by accusing God. In what ways have you tried to make sense of your pain by subtly positioning yourself as right and God as wrong?

_____
_____
_____
_____
_____
_____
_____
_____
_____
_____

We're reminded that "God is more than the people at church." How does that truth challenge your assumptions, especially if your church experience has left you skeptical or bitter?

_____
_____
_____
_____
_____
_____
_____
_____
_____
_____
_____
_____
_____

CHAPTER 5

GOD CARES

Your goal should be for God to make things right, not punish whoever hurt you.

REVIEW, REFLECT, AND RESPOND

> **READING TIME** As you read Chapter 5: "God Cares" in *Church Hurt*, review, reflect on, and respond to the text by answering the following questions.

What memories or emotions are still "sticking" to you—and how have they affected your faith or behavior?

_____
_____
_____
_____
_____
_____
_____
_____

The chapter reminds us that God hears our "cries of distress"—even when no one else does. What's a moment when you doubted that anyone, including God, truly saw or cared about your hurt?

_____
_____
_____
_____
_____
_____
_____
_____

> *"When he looked out over the crowds, his heart broke. So confused and aimless they were, like sheep with no shepherd."* — Matthew 9:36 (MSG)

Consider the scripture above and answer the following questions:

What recent situation has made you feel "confused and aimless"? How might Jesus be inviting you to experience His shepherding care there?

_____
_____
_____
_____
_____
_____

How have you underestimated the emotional connection God has to your suffering—especially when that suffering came from His people?

_____
_____
_____
_____
_____
_____

In the story of Cain and Abel, God says Abel's blood cried out for justice. What "cry" is still coming from your heart—and how do you need to bring that to God, rather than trying to silence or suppress it?

_____
_____
_____
_____
_____
_____
_____
_____
_____
_____

God may give people time to repent instead of punishing them immediately. When has it been difficult for you to accept God's patience with someone who hurt you? What does that reveal about your desire for justice or revenge?

_____
_____
_____
_____
_____
_____
_____
_____
_____
_____

Your goal should be for God to make things right—not punish whoever hurt you. Have you confused those two? How has that mindset affected your healing?

When have you expected God to act more like an impersonal judge than a caring father? How has that expectation shaped your willingness to trust Him?

How does the father-heart image of God challenge or affirm your current understanding of how God sees and responds to your pain?

_____
_____
_____
_____
_____
_____
_____
_____
_____
_____

If God's thoughts about you outnumber the grains of sand, what does that say about the worth of your healing—and the care He's already extending to you?

_____
_____
_____
_____
_____
_____
_____
_____
_____
_____

CHAPTER 6

LET GOD HEAL YOU

Your goal should be for God to make things right, not punish whoever hurt you.

REVIEW, REFLECT, AND RESPOND

READING TIME As you read Chapter 6: "Let God Heal You" in *Church Hurt*, review, reflect on, and respond to the text by answering the following questions.

What internal script do you keep rehearsing that convinces you your pain is permanent—or that healing is for others, but not for you?

_____
_____
_____
_____
_____
_____
_____
_____

Butler says there comes a moment when the hurt feels like it never happened. Does that idea scare you, comfort you, or feel impossible right now? Why?

_____
_____
_____
_____
_____
_____
_____
_____

> *"All praise to God, the Father of our Lord Jesus Christ. God is our merciful Father and the source of all comfort. He comforts us in all our troubles so that we can comfort others. When they are troubled, we will be able to give them the same comfort God has given us."*
> 2 Corinthians 1:2-4 (NLT)

Consider the scripture above and answer the following questions:

Where have you been waiting to feel different before believing God has answered your prayer for comfort? How does this scripture challenge that approach?

_____
_____
_____
_____
_____
_____

God comforts us not only to heal us—but so we can comfort others. Who might need the same comfort you've received (or are still learning to receive)?

_____
_____
_____
_____
_____
_____
_____

The chapter warns that ignoring our brokenness doesn't lead to healing. What's one area you've tried to bury or minimize instead of inviting God into it?

___

This chapter gives a practical prayer for comfort: asking God in faith and receiving it like you would an Amazon order. How comfortable are you with praying that way—and what stops you from doing it?

___

The story of the woman who lost her husband illustrates how God provides supernatural peace, even in devastating circumstances. When has God's comfort met you in a moment of deep loss or instability?

_____
_____
_____
_____
_____
_____
_____
_____
_____
_____
_____

Think about something you once thought you'd never recover from. What evidence do you see that healing has already begun—or that God is still inviting you to cooperate with the process?

_____
_____
_____
_____
_____
_____
_____
_____
_____
_____
_____

The chapter ends with the image of Paul writing about joy while standing in sewage. What does that story reveal about the power of God's comfort, even when your situation doesn't change right away?

_____
_____
_____
_____
_____
_____
_____
_____
_____
_____

What's one bold declaration you can start making—not based on how you feel, but based on the truth that God has comforted and is healing you?

_____
_____
_____
_____
_____
_____
_____
_____
_____
_____

CHAPTER 7

LET IT GO!

Unforgiveness is like drinking poison
and expecting the other person to die.

REVIEW, REFLECT, AND RESPOND

READING TIME As you read Chapter 7: "Let It Go!" in *Church Hurt*, review, reflect on, and respond to the text by answering the following questions.

All prisoners have a release date. Who have you mentally or emotionally kept locked up—and how long have they been serving time in your heart?

_____
_____
_____
_____
_____
_____
_____
_____

When have you offered partial forgiveness—releasing some of the offense, but holding onto a sliver of blame or control? What impact has that 10 percent had on your peace and healing?

_____
_____
_____
_____
_____
_____
_____
_____

> *"But when you are praying, first forgive anyone you are holding a grudge against, so that your Father in heaven will forgive your sins, too."* — Mark 11:25 (NLT)

Consider the scripture above and answer the following questions:

According to Jesus, forgiveness is a prerequisite to receiving from God. What prayers might be hindered in your life because of lingering unforgiveness?

_____
_____
_____
_____
_____
_____
_____

The command to forgive includes "anyone." Who is the person you've tried to exclude from that category, and why?

_____
_____
_____
_____
_____
_____
_____

The parable in Matthew 18 reminds us that we've been forgiven of far more than we've been hurt. How often do you reflect on God's grace toward you when you're struggling to forgive someone else?

___

The balloon imagery in this chapter is powerful—visualizing your grudge and letting it float away. If you were to name one specific grudge you've been gripping tightly, what would it be?

___

How has holding onto a grudge shaped your identity, outlook, or ability to experience joy? What would change if you finally let it go—for good?

_____
_____
_____
_____
_____
_____
_____
_____
_____
_____
_____

What grudge have you spiritualized or justified as "righteous anger" but now recognize as unforgiveness?

_____
_____
_____
_____
_____
_____
_____
_____
_____
_____
_____

Forgiveness doesn't always mean reconciliation, but it does mean release. What boundaries or mindset shifts might help you forgive someone even if the relationship never returns to what it was?

_____
_____
_____
_____
_____
_____
_____
_____
_____
_____
_____
_____
_____

CHAPTER 8

DON'T PICK THE SCAB

Decide to let what's dead be dead; don't die with the dead.

REVIEW, REFLECT, AND RESPOND

READING TIME As you read Chapter 8: "Don't Pick the Scab" in *Church Hurt*, review, reflect on, and respond to the text by answering the following questions.

What behaviors, conversations, or thought patterns have you used to reopen wounds that were beginning to heal?

_____
_____
_____
_____
_____
_____
_____
_____
_____

The chapter challenges us to "change the channel" in our minds. What's one specific thought or narrative you need to replace with something true, lovely, or praise-worthy?

_____
_____
_____
_____
_____
_____
_____
_____
_____

> *"I know what I'm doing. I have it all planned out—plans to take care of you, not abandon you, plans to give you the future you hoped for."*   Jeremiah 29:11-12 (MSG)

Consider the scripture above and answer the following questions:

What part of this promise do you struggle to believe when you're stuck in the pain of church hurt—God's plan, His nearness, or His care?

_____
_____
_____
_____
_____
_____
_____

How has dwelling on the past kept you from embracing the future God still has planned for you? Be honest—do you believe His plans are good?

_____
_____
_____
_____
_____
_____
_____
_____

Jesus forgave those crucifying Him in the moment—before they apologized. What step toward forgiveness might you need to take, even if reconciliation never comes?

_____
_____
_____
_____
_____
_____
_____
_____
_____
_____

The Church is also a source of healing, not just hurt. When have you experienced a word, message, or person from the Church being used by God to restore you?

_____
_____
_____
_____
_____
_____
_____
_____
_____
_____

What's one reason you've been tempted to disconnect from church—and what's one reason to reconnect, based on the healing and encouragement God can still provide through it?

_____
_____
_____
_____
_____
_____
_____
_____
_____
_____

Think about a time when someone said exactly what you needed to hear. How might God be inviting you to stay connected so you don't miss those divine appointments?

_____
_____
_____
_____
_____
_____
_____
_____
_____
_____

When you think about the way you retell your story—whether to others or in your own mind—does it lead to healing or reinforce your identity as a victim? If you could reframe your story right now, what would that sound like?

_____
_____
_____
_____
_____
_____
_____
_____
_____
_____

CHAPTER 9

TIME TO GROW

If it's evil, add a D; that means it's from the devil. If it's good, eliminate an O; that means it's from God.

REVIEW, REFLECT, AND RESPOND

> **READING TIME** As you read Chapter 9: "Time to Grow" in *Church Hurt*, review, reflect on, and respond to the text by answering the following questions.

Spiritual immaturity is like a fifteen-year-old still needing baby food. What is one spiritual behavior, reaction, or belief that no longer fits who you are becoming?

_____
_____
_____
_____
_____
_____

In the parable of the sower, Satan strips God's Word from the heart through offense. When has resentment or touchiness kept you from experiencing the fruit of what God was trying to grow in you?

_____
_____
_____
_____
_____
_____

> *"You have been believers so long now that you ought to be teaching others. Instead, you need someone to teach you again the basic things about God's word. You are like babies who need milk and cannot eat solid food."* — Hebrews 5:12 (NLT)

Consider the scripture above and answer the following questions:

What's one area in your faith where you know you've been coasting on the basics (milk) rather than pressing into growth (solid food)?

_____
_____
_____
_____
_____
_____
_____

How might your healing journey be stuck—not because God hasn't moved but because you haven't grown into what He's already provided?

_____
_____
_____
_____
_____
_____
_____

Church people aren't perfect and never will be. How has expecting perfection from others set you up for disappointment—and how might grace change your expectations?

_____
_____
_____
_____
_____
_____
_____
_____
_____
_____
_____

What's a spiritual "myth" you've believed—about church, God, or people—that it's time to outgrow for good?

_____
_____
_____
_____
_____
_____
_____
_____
_____
_____
_____

The "D for devil, O for God" filter is a simple but powerful tool. Looking at recent experiences, where have you confused the source of your pain—and what truth do you need to reclaim?

_____
_____
_____
_____
_____
_____
_____
_____
_____
_____
_____
_____

What excuse have you been using to justify spiritual immaturity—and how long has that excuse kept you stuck?

_____
_____
_____
_____
_____
_____
_____
_____
_____
_____
_____
_____

If someone else acted the way you've been acting—touchy, resentful, easily offended—would you call it spiritual maturity? Why or why not? What would you expect from that person instead?

_____
_____
_____
_____
_____
_____
_____
_____
_____

If you were to fully take ownership of your spiritual growth, what practical change would you start making this week—in thought, habit, or attitude?

_____
_____
_____
_____
_____
_____
_____
_____
_____

CHAPTER 10

THE CHURCH IS FULL OF HYPOCRITES!

When we keep our eyes on Jesus and grow in Him, we don't have time to see the mistakes of others.

REVIEW, REFLECT, AND RESPOND

> **READING TIME** As you read Chapter 10: "The Church Is Full of Hypocrites!" in *Church Hurt*, review, reflect on, and respond to the text by answering the following questions.

What area of your own life needs the same mercy and patience you've been reluctant to extend to someone else?

_____
_____
_____
_____
_____
_____
_____
_____

What excuses have you made for avoiding church, and what are they really protecting you from?

_____
_____
_____
_____
_____
_____
_____
_____

> *"Dear brothers and sisters, if another believer is overcome by some sin, you who are godly should gently and humbly help that person back onto the right path. And be careful not to fall into the same temptation yourself."*
>
> Galatians 6:1 (NLT)

Consider the scripture above and answer the following questions:

When have you responded with criticism instead of compassion to someone else's failure in the church? What could gentle restoration have looked like instead?

_____
_____
_____
_____
_____
_____

Why do you think God pairs restoration with humility in this passage? How does this correct your own approach to other believers' weaknesses?

_____
_____
_____
_____
_____
_____
_____

How has your focus on others' failures distracted you from tending to your own spiritual growth? Be specific.

_____
_____
_____
_____
_____
_____
_____
_____
_____
_____

When you think about people who've hurt you in church, have you judged their character or just their behavior? What's the difference, and why does it matter?

_____
_____
_____
_____
_____
_____
_____
_____
_____
_____
_____

What's one example of when you were tempted to leave or disengage from a church community because of someone else's sin? Looking back, what did you learn—or miss—by how you handled it?

_____
_____
_____
_____
_____
_____
_____
_____
_____

The chapter calls out the "social media mob" mentality. When have you been part of that mob—either online or in conversation—and what might repentance look like for that?

_____
_____
_____
_____
_____
_____
_____
_____
_____
_____
_____
_____

What would shift in your heart if you approached hypocrites in the church as future testimonies instead of permanent disappointments?

___

CHAPTER 11

THE YELLOW BRICK ROAD

Don't want that sin so bad
that you couldn't care less
about God or His church.

REVIEW, REFLECT, AND RESPOND

READING TIME As you read Chapter 11: "The Yellow Brick Road" in *Church Hurt*, review, reflect on, and respond to the text by answering the following questions.

What voices or influences in your life have made you believe that holiness is restrictive rather than protective?

_____
_____
_____
_____
_____
_____
_____
_____

This chapter compares holiness to a yellow brick road—a path that leads to safety, joy, and purpose. What temptation or habit is luring you off that road today?

_____
_____
_____
_____
_____
_____
_____
_____

> *"There is a way that seems right to a man, but the end of it is death."*   Proverbs 14:12 (author paraphrase)

Consider the scripture above and answer the following questions:

When have you been convinced that your way was right, only to realize later it led to harm or regret?

_____
_____
_____
_____
_____
_____
_____
_____

In what area of life have you ignored warning signs from God or others—and what consequences followed?

_____
_____
_____
_____
_____
_____
_____
_____

Think about a time when you wanted validation more than truth. How did that desire impact your view of God, church, or correction?

_____
_____
_____
_____
_____
_____
_____
_____
_____
_____
_____
_____

This chapter says that sin doesn't always pay immediately, but it always pays eventually. What "wages" of sin have you seen play out in your own life or the lives of others?

_____
_____
_____
_____
_____
_____
_____
_____
_____
_____
_____
_____

When have you mistaken your resistance to God's standards as "church hurt"? How can you tell the difference between being hurt by people and convicted by truth?

___

There are several biblical figures named who were flawed but still used by God. How does that challenge your excuses or hesitation about returning to church or submitting to God's ways?

___

If you were completely honest, what part of your current lifestyle would you rather defend than surrender—and what's the real cost of holding onto it?

___

CHAPTER 12

IS CHURCH REALLY NECESSARY?

You don't do life alone and have success.

REVIEW, REFLECT, AND RESPOND

> **READING TIME** As you read Chapter 12: "Is Church Really Necessary?" in *Church Hurt*, review, reflect on, and respond to the text by answering the following questions.

This chapter says church is God's idea—not man's. When have you treated church as optional or man-made? What led to that mindset?

_____
_____
_____
_____
_____
_____
_____
_____

What's one specific way your spiritual growth has stalled or regressed since pulling away from church community?

_____
_____
_____
_____
_____
_____
_____
_____

"Two people are better off than one, for they can help each other succeed. If one person falls, the other can reach out and help. But someone who falls alone is in real trouble. Likewise, two people lying close together can keep each other warm. But how can one be warm alone? A person standing alone can be attacked and defeated, but two can stand back-to-back and conquer. Three are even better, for a triple-braided cord is not easily broken.".   Ecclesiastes 4:9-12 (NLT)

Consider the scripture above and answer the following questions:

What benefits of community in this passage have you missed out on by choosing distance over connection in response to church hurt?

_____
_____
_____
_____
_____

Where in your life have you felt spiritually attacked or defeated—and how might reengaging with church community help you stand stronger?

_____
_____
_____
_____
_____

"God doesn't send people to church—He sends them to a pastor." What does that mean to you, and how does that idea challenge your assumptions about leadership and spiritual authority?

_____
_____
_____
_____
_____
_____

Have you ever left a church before God released you? Why, and how did you know it was your decision and not God's?

_____
_____
_____
_____
_____
_____

The chapter makes clear that God's plan includes community, not independence. What fear, pride, or past wound has made you suspicious of that plan?

_____
_____
_____
_____
_____
_____

Are you willing to risk spiritual stagnation just to keep control of your story? What might God be asking you to surrender so you can be joined to the body of Christ, not just "saved" from your sin?

_____
_____
_____
_____
_____
_____
_____
_____
_____
_____
_____

In what ways have you been expecting to receive the full blessing and purposes of God while staying disconnected from the church family He designed to be part of the process?

_____
_____
_____
_____
_____
_____
_____
_____
_____
_____
_____

Have you ever faced a difficult season and realized too late that you'd pulled away from the very people who could have supported you? What assumptions or fears caused you to pull away in the first place—and did they hold up when life got hard?

_____
_____
_____
_____
_____
_____
_____
_____
_____
_____
_____
_____

CHAPTER 13

IS CHURCH ATTENDANCE OPTIONAL?

God didn't abuse you. God didn't send those people to you. That's not a God thing. That's a people thing.

REVIEW, REFLECT, AND RESPOND

READING TIME As you read Chapter 13: "Is Church Attendance Optional?" in *Church Hurt*, review, reflect on, and respond to the text by answering the following questions.

The chapter compares neglecting church to skipping out on dates with someone you claim to love. What does your church attendance—or lack of it—say about your relationship with or view of God?

_____
_____
_____
_____
_____
_____
_____
_____

What are you blaming God for that someone in church did? How has that misplaced blame affected your connection to Him?

_____
_____
_____
_____
_____
_____
_____

"Come close to God, and God will come close to you."
James 4:8 (NLT)

Consider the scripture above and answer the following questions:

What does the phrase "come close to God" mean to you in light of your current relationship with the church—and how might church attendance be part of that pursuit?

_____
_____
_____
_____
_____
_____
_____

The verse says God draws near in response to us drawing near to Him. How does that challenge the idea that God should pursue us while we remain distant?

_____
_____
_____
_____
_____
_____
_____

When you withhold yourself from church because of past hurt, who might be missing the blessing of your presence, encouragement, or example?

_____
_____
_____
_____
_____
_____
_____
_____
_____
_____

This chapter confronts the idea that you're "cool with God" while staying disconnected from church. Where might that mindset be rooted more in convenience than conviction?

_____
_____
_____
_____
_____
_____
_____
_____
_____
_____

Jesus went to church, even though He knew He'd be betrayed by people in the pews. What excuse are you holding onto that He didn't?

Church is described as a hospital full of "ex-somethings"—including you. How does that truth reshape your expectations of church people and your place among them?

What's your biggest fear about returning to church or attending more consistently—and how does a biblical understanding of the body of Christ and your role in it confront that fear?

_____
_____
_____
_____
_____
_____
_____
_____
_____
_____
_____
_____
_____

CHAPTER 14

I DON'T NEED A LEADER

Where you go to church is a
matter of life and death!

REVIEW, REFLECT, AND RESPOND

READING TIME As you read Chapter 14: "I Don't Need a Leader" in *Church Hurt*, review, reflect on, and respond to the text by answering the following questions.

When you think of submitting to a spiritual leader, what emotions surface—and what personal experiences might be fueling that reaction?

_____
_____
_____
_____
_____
_____
_____
_____

Have you ever equated correction from a spiritual leader with rejection? How might that misunderstanding be keeping you from growth and protection?

_____
_____
_____
_____
_____
_____
_____
_____

> *"Obey your spiritual leaders, and do what they say. Their work is to watch over your souls, and they are accountable to God. Give them reason to do this with joy and not with sorrow. That would certainly not be for your benefit."* — Hebrews 13:17 (NLT)

Consider the scripture above and answer the following questions:

According to this verse, spiritual leaders are accountable to God for watching over your soul. How do you reconcile this with your experiences, and how does this truth challenge them?

_____
_____
_____
_____
_____
_____

The verse says resisting spiritual leadership "would certainly not be for your benefit." In light of your church hurt, how might holding onto mistrust be hurting you more than protecting you?

_____
_____
_____
_____
_____
_____

God doesn't ask us to follow perfect leaders—just the ones He's assigned. How have you let a leader's flaws justify your disobedience to God's structure? Explain.

___

The chapter says your pastor may hold the answer, breakthrough, or wisdom you've been praying for. Have you stayed close enough to receive it—or have you stepped out from under the "shower head"?

___

When have you seen firsthand—either in your own life or someone else's—that being connected to the right spiritual leadership is a matter of life and death? How did that moment reshape your view of church?

_____
_____
_____
_____
_____
_____
_____
_____
_____
_____

Has church hurt caused you to see all spiritual leaders through the lens of one painful experience? How might that filter be distorting the voice of the ones God has assigned to help heal you?

_____
_____
_____
_____
_____
_____
_____
_____
_____
_____

If someone in your life said, "I don't need a leader," how would you respond now, after reading this chapter?

_____
_____
_____
_____
_____
_____
_____
_____
_____
_____
_____
_____
_____
_____

CHAPTER 15

IT HAPPENS

God believes you are better off
in a church where somebody
might hurt you from time to
time than out of church.

REVIEW, REFLECT, AND RESPOND

> **READING TIME** As you read Chapter 15: "It Happens" in *Church Hurt*, review, reflect on, and respond to the text by answering the following questions.

This chapter says, "God already knew what would happen to you in church and still sent you there." How does that truth challenge the belief that your pain disqualifies God's plan?

_____
_____
_____
_____
_____
_____
_____
_____

Have you ever expected people in church to behave better than people in the world—and then felt betrayed when they didn't? If you were to challenge that belief, how would you do it?

_____
_____
_____
_____
_____
_____
_____
_____

> *"Always be humble and gentle. Be patient with each other, making allowance for each other's faults because of your love. Make every effort to keep yourselves united in the Spirit, binding yourselves together with peace."*
> Ephesians 4:2-3 (NLT)

Consider the scripture above and answer the following questions:

What does it mean to "bind yourself together with peace," especially in a place where conflict or disappointment has occurred?

_____
_____
_____
_____
_____
_____
_____

In your healing journey, where is God inviting you to practice humility, gentleness, or patience toward the very people who've hurt you? What would that look like?

_____
_____
_____
_____
_____
_____
_____

Think about the worst moment of church hurt you've experienced. If you were the one who caused that kind of pain—intentionally or not—how would you hope others would view you, and how does that perspective shift the way you see the person who hurt you?

_____
_____
_____
_____
_____
_____
_____
_____
_____
_____

The book says church is like a hospital—full of sick people being treated, not perfect people pretending to be whole. Where have you been holding people to a standard you don't always meet yourself?

_____
_____
_____
_____
_____
_____
_____
_____
_____
_____

Have you ever punished your current church—or your future one—for the failures of your past one? What has that cost you?

_____
_____
_____
_____
_____
_____
_____
_____
_____
_____

If you only show up when things are perfect, will you ever experience the kind of deep, grace-filled connection that can only happen when it's messy?

_____
_____
_____
_____
_____
_____
_____
_____
_____
_____
_____

What would it look like to stop using pain as a reason to stay away—and start using love as a reason to return?

_____
_____
_____
_____
_____
_____
_____
_____
_____
_____
_____
_____
_____
_____
_____

CHAPTER 16

FRIENDLY FIRE

Many take on the responsibility
of the apostle Paul when they
are the apostle of none!

REVIEW, REFLECT, AND RESPOND

> **READING TIME** As you read Chapter 16: "Friendly Fire" in *Church Hurt*, review, reflect on, and respond to the text by answering the following questions.

Have you ever joined in on criticizing a church or leader because it felt justified or popular? Looking back, what do you wish you had done differently?

_____
_____
_____
_____
_____
_____
_____
_____

This chapter calls "church bashing" a tool of the enemy. How does that shift your perspective on conversations you've had or posts you've shared?

_____
_____
_____
_____
_____
_____
_____
_____

> *"But Jesus knew their thoughts, and said to them, 'Every kingdom divided against itself is brought to desolation, and every city or house divided against itself will not stand."* — Matthew 12:25 (NKJV)

Consider the scripture above and answer the following questions:

According to this verse, what happens when division goes unchecked in the church? How have you seen this play out in your own experience with church hurt?

_____
_____
_____
_____
_____
_____
_____

In what ways might criticizing the church—rather than constructively contributing to it—be making you part of the problem Jesus warned about?

_____
_____
_____
_____
_____
_____
_____

When you reflect on the times you've judged another ministry or leader, were you genuinely seeking restoration—or were you just venting frustration or pride?

Have you ever been tempted to believe that calling out wrong is the same as standing for truth? How do you discern the difference between righteous correction and self-righteous criticism?

This chapter challenges us to consider our "spiritual jurisdiction." Where have you stepped outside of your role in trying to correct someone God never asked you to?

_____
_____
_____
_____
_____
_____
_____
_____
_____
_____

Consider a time when someone else's sin or doctrinal differences stirred anger or superiority in you. How could humility have changed your response?

_____
_____
_____
_____
_____
_____
_____
_____
_____
_____

What's one step you can take this week to repair division and build unity in your corner of the Church?

_____
_____
_____
_____
_____
_____
_____
_____
_____
_____
_____
_____
_____
_____

CHAPTER 17

CHURCH ISN'T WACK

When people start messing with you, just stretch your wings out and go higher.

REVIEW, REFLECT, AND RESPOND

READING TIME As you read Chapter 17: "Church Isn't Wack" in *Church Hurt*, review, reflect on, and respond to the text by answering the following questions.

Have you ever experienced or witnessed something supernatural at church—and how does that memory challenge or align with your view of church today?

_____
_____
_____
_____
_____
_____
_____
_____

"Church isn't wack. It's awesome." What moments or stories from your life contradict that statement—and how might God want to reframe them?

_____
_____
_____
_____
_____
_____
_____
_____
_____
_____

> *"'It isn't right to take food from the children and throw it to the dogs.' She replied, 'That's true, Lord, but even dogs are allowed to eat the scraps that fall beneath their master's table.' 'Dear woman,' Jesus said to her, 'your faith is great. Your request is granted.' And her daughter was instantly healed."* Matthew 15:26-28 (NLT)

Consider the scripture above and answer the following questions:

What does this scripture teach you about staying engaged with God and His people—even when it feels like you're being overlooked or misunderstood?

_____
_____
_____
_____
_____
_____

How does the woman's story challenge you to keep showing up in spiritual community, even after experiencing hurt?

_____
_____
_____
_____
_____
_____

The book compares being easily offended at church to being "touchy." When was the last time you got offended in church—and what was driving that sensitivity?

_____
_____
_____
_____
_____
_____
_____
_____
_____
_____

The woman at the well, Hannah, and the woman Jesus called a dog all had reasons to walk away hurt. But they stayed, and God met them there. What might you be missing out on if you keep walking away?

_____
_____
_____
_____
_____
_____
_____
_____
_____
_____

Have you ever watched someone make a mistake in church and been quick to judge or criticize instead of helping them get restored? How could your response be different next time?

_____
_____
_____
_____
_____
_____
_____
_____
_____
_____

How might God be asking you to stop engaging with petty offense and instead rise above it?

_____
_____
_____
_____
_____
_____
_____
_____
_____
_____

What instruction from the "church manual" have you been ignoring, and how is that affecting your experience of church life?

___

CHAPTER 18

FOR PASTORS ONLY

Ultimately, we serve in ministry for God, not people.

REVIEW, REFLECT, AND RESPOND

READING TIME As you read Chapter 18: "For Pastors Only" in *Church Hurt*, review, reflect on, and respond to the text by answering the following questions.

What part of your calling has felt most costly because of the wounds you've received in ministry?

_____
_____
_____
_____
_____
_____
_____
_____
_____

What internal conversations have you had with God about quitting—and how has He responded?

_____
_____
_____
_____
_____
_____
_____
_____
_____

"For we speak as messengers approved by God to be entrusted with the Good News. Our purpose is to please God, not people. He alone examines the motives of our hearts.". 1 Thessalonians 2:4 (NLT)

Consider the scripture above and answer the following questions:

How has the pressure to please people in your church ever pulled you away from your purpose?

_____
_____
_____
_____
_____
_____
_____

If God alone examines the motives of your heart, how does that truth help reframe the pain of being misunderstood or falsely accused by others?

_____
_____
_____
_____
_____
_____
_____

Have you ever caught yourself avoiding deep connection with your congregation to protect yourself from future pain? What have you done about it?

What beliefs about ministry or leadership have shifted because of betrayal or slander?

How have you handled situations where the people you helped the most became your harshest critics?

_____
_____
_____
_____
_____
_____
_____
_____
_____
_____

What spiritual or emotional "limps" do you carry—and how do you lead from that place of vulnerability?

_____
_____
_____
_____
_____
_____
_____
_____
_____
_____
_____

What might change in your ministry if your focus fully shifted from avoiding hurt to pleasing God alone?

_____
_____
_____
_____
_____
_____
_____
_____
_____
_____
_____
_____
_____
_____
_____

CHAPTER 19

CHURCH HURT AND PREACHERS' KIDS

> PKs are known for running from church, and although it's often because of church people, too much of the time, it's because of their parents.

REVIEW, REFLECT, AND RESPOND

READING TIME As you read Chapter 19: "Church Hurt and Preachers' Kids" in *Church Hurt*, review, reflect on, and respond to the text by answering the following questions.

What's a moment in your childhood where you felt like ministry came before you—and how has that shaped your relationship with both church and family?

_____
_____
_____
_____
_____
_____
_____
_____

Have you ever found yourself angry at church people when, deep down, the root of that pain was actually a parent who wasn't present?

_____
_____
_____
_____
_____
_____
_____
_____

> *"If another believer sins against you, go privately and point out the offense. If the other person listens and confesses it, you have won that person back."*
>
> Matthew 18:15 (NLT)

Consider the scripture above and answer the following questions:

What fears or assumptions might keep you from having an honest, private conversation with your parent or someone else about how their ministry choices hurt you?

_____
_____
_____
_____
_____
_____
_____

If you could share one offense with your offender without fear of rejection or defensiveness, what would it be—and what outcome would you hope for?

_____
_____
_____
_____
_____
_____
_____

Have you ever felt like "collateral damage," and if so, how has that affected your ability to trust church leaders or spiritual authority today?

In what ways has your past made it easier to read people—and harder to open up to them?

Have you ever used your knowledge of church culture as a shield to stay close enough to look spiritual but distant enough not to get hurt again? What has this distance cost you?

_____
_____
_____
_____
_____
_____
_____
_____
_____
_____

What would it take for you to release your parents from expectations they failed to meet—and how would that free you to heal?

_____
_____
_____
_____
_____
_____
_____
_____
_____
_____

If your calling mirrors your parents' calling, what baggage are you carrying that might sabotage your own ministry if left unaddressed?

_____
_____
_____
_____
_____
_____
_____
_____
_____
_____
_____
_____
_____
_____

CHAPTER 20

CHURCH HURT AND FAMILY MINISTRY

> One mistake we make too often in ministry is staying married to our methods rather than to the message.

REVIEW, REFLECT, AND RESPOND

READING TIME As you read Chapter 20: "Church Hurt and Family Ministry" in *Church Hurt*, review, reflect on, and respond to the text by answering the following questions.

What part of your child's calling challenges your need for control, legacy, or affirmation?

___

Have you ever confused your child's obedience to God with disobedience to you? How did that impact your relationship?

___

"So after more fasting and prayer, the men laid their hands on them and sent them on their way."

Acts 13:3 (NLT)

Consider the scripture above and answer the following questions:

What does this verse teach you about the importance of releasing your child into ministry rather than controlling their assignment?

_____
_____
_____
_____
_____
_____
_____

What fears or insecurities might be keeping you from truly sending your children "on their way"?

_____
_____
_____
_____
_____
_____
_____
_____

In what ways might you be unintentionally prioritizing your ministry's future over your child's personal growth or marital health?

Do you truly honor your child's spiritual authority and anointing—or do you view them only as your son or daughter? How do you know?

If your child's calling takes them away from your ministry, how will you celebrate that as a win for the Kingdom instead of a loss for your church or organization?

What unresolved hurt from your own past might be shaping how you handle your child's role in ministry?

Are you willing to let your child "wear their own armor"? What steps can you take today to give them room to lead in the way God uniquely designed them?

_____
_____
_____
_____
_____
_____
_____
_____
_____
_____
_____
_____
_____

CHAPTER 21

WHEN A LEADER FAILS

Not going to church because a minister may fall is like never flying again in a plane due to a fear of crashing.

REVIEW, REFLECT, AND RESPOND

READING TIME As you read Chapter 21: "When a Leader Fails" in *Church Hurt*, review, reflect on, and respond to the text by answering the following questions.

"Then the churches throughout all Judea, Galilee, and Samaria had peace and were edified. And walking in the fear of the Lord and in the comfort of the Holy Spirit, they were multiplied."   Acts 9:31 (NKJV)

Consider the scripture above and answer the following questions:

How does this verse challenge the idea that the church can't thrive after failure?

_____
_____
_____
_____
_____
_____
_____
_____
_____
_____
_____
_____

What would it look like for you to walk in "the fear of the Lord" instead of the fear of what broken leaders might do again?

When a leader fell in your life, how did it impact your relationship with God—did you separate your faith from the failure, or did they become intertwined?

This chapter says, "God doesn't give up on fallen leaders as easily as we do." How do you reconcile that truth with your own tendency to cancel or distance yourself?

___

In what ways have you carried the pain of a leader's fall like a wound you refuse to let God touch?

___

Have you ever used someone else's moral failure as a permission slip to disengage, delay your own calling, or lower your standards? What were you thinking at the time, and how has that thinking changed since then?

_____

_____

_____

_____

_____

_____

_____

_____

_____

_____

What might honoring a fallen leader look like—even if you never speak to them again?

_____

_____

_____

_____

_____

_____

_____

_____

_____

_____

CHAPTER 22

IT'S TIME TO MOVE PAST CHURCH HURT

> Let God heal you, let God mature you, and let God use you to help others in this world.

REVIEW, REFLECT, AND RESPOND

READING TIME As you read Chapter 22: "It's Time to Move Past Church Hurt" in *Church Hurt*, review, reflect on, and respond to the text by answering the following questions.

Looking back over this journey, what truths or insights about God, the Church, or yourself have stood out to you the most?

_____
_____
_____
_____
_____
_____
_____
_____

In what ways has this book challenged or changed the story you've been telling yourself about your church hurt?

_____
_____
_____
_____
_____
_____
_____
_____

How likely are you to return to church or become fully engaged again?

_____
_____
_____
_____
_____
_____
_____
_____
_____
_____
_____

What practical steps will you take to move forward—not just in forgiveness, but in fully embracing your role in God's plan?

_____
_____
_____
_____
_____
_____
_____
_____
_____
_____
_____
_____

Who in your life needs to hear your testimony—not just of pain, but of healing and hope?

_____
_____
_____
_____
_____
_____
_____
_____
_____
_____
_____
_____
_____
_____

www.ingramcontent.com/pod-product-compliance
Lightning Source LLC
Chambersburg PA
CBHW062113080426
42734CB00012B/2851

This companion study guide to *Church Hurt: It's Time to Heal* walks with you through the often-painful process of acknowledging wounds, confronting hard truths, and rediscovering hope after hurt within the church. Designed for personal reflection or group discussion, each session blends biblical insight, practical wisdom, and space for honest processing, to help you move from pain to wholeness without losing your faith in God.

Through guided questions and Scripture engagement, you'll identify the root causes of church hurt, recognize the enemy's role in division, and learn how to navigate offense with both grace and wisdom.

This journey isn't about ignoring what happened—it's about walking toward the One who never failed you.

Whether your wounds are fresh or years old, this study guide will help you find restoration, reclaim joy in your faith community, and move forward with emotional and spiritual strength.

Healing begins here.

With an undeniable passion for equipping others to experience the future God has for them, André Butler is on a mission to share God's desire to prosper His people in every area of their lives—and His call for them to help win the world to Jesus.

As the pastor of Faith Xperience Church (FX Church) in the heart of Detroit, he is a sought-after conference speaker and host known for his practical and relatable approach to preaching God's Word. A graduate of Rhema Bible Training Center, Pastor André also holds a bachelor's degree in Management from Kennesaw State University. He resides in metro Detroit.

André connects regularly with followers on Instagram, TikTok, X, and Facebook. His messages can be found on his YouTube channel and at AndreButler.com.